From ... with ...

SHE SHALL
BE CALLED
WOMAN

Marie Holt

Marie Holt

AXIOM
PRESS

Mobile, Alabama

ISBN 978-1-58169-667-7
For Worldwide Distribution
Printed in the U.S.A.
Axiom Press
P.O. Box 191540 • Mobile, AL 36619

Table of Contents

For Barry

And all the girls

in my life

Introduction

For many years I have dreamed that somewhere inside me was some sort of writing waiting to escape. At one time I pursued my dream and attempted to write a novel, a love story with emphasis on the life of today. However, I don't live life in the fast lane, and I soon discovered this was not the path for any writing I might do. As neither my heart nor my mind were in it, I let this dream go.

My professional background is in education, and I considered writing a children's literature book. However all the good ideas seemed to have been taken, and to add to that I don't do cutesy. With my dream slowly fading, I had almost given up when something extraordinary happened.

For the past several years the deacons of my church, St. Mark Presbyterian in Ballwin, Missouri, have sponsored a Christmas House Tour with the proceeds going to Lydia's House, an organization that protects and aids abused women and their children. The tour had been very successful, but as it happens, interest had waned, and it was time to come up with a new idea.

A committee of seven women, myself included, met to brainstorm new ideas, and out of our ideas began the plans to offer a Christmas Tea in the beautiful narthex of our church. As our plans progressed, our chairperson suggested that a devotion seemed appropriate and perhaps our associate minister would take that responsibility. Suddenly I said that I would be honored to take that responsibility. It was almost as if someone were speaking for me as I had absolutely no idea what I would say or do.

A few weeks later I had given no thought to the devotion, but one night as I lay awake in the comfort of my bed, my mind began working and I knew exactly what I would say and do. Again it was almost as if someone were thinking for me. It also occurred to me that perhaps my writing dream could become a reality as well with the ideas forming in my mind.

For the devotion I did a first person narrative (in costume) telling the Christmas story from the innkeeper's wife's point of view. I concluded my narrative by relating how women of today can and do experience the same feelings as she did. She is not mentioned in the Bible but she had to have been there right beside her husband doing her part to help. And she had a strong message to share.

My goal for my writing is twofold. First, I have reached into the lives of unnamed and sometimes unmentioned women in the Bible. Often the biblical reference of the unnamed woman is brief, and I have taken that reference and tried to slip into the persona of that woman by telling her story as I imagine it could have happened.

Second, I have used the stories of these woman, both unnamed and unmentioned, to offer encouragement and peace to women of today who might find themselves in similar circumstances.

So often my personal devotions tell me that God is able to do far beyond all that I ask or imagine. I should come to him with positive expectations and know that there is no limit to what I can accomplish. So with God by my side, I am ready to share my dream. Come with me, and I hope you might be touched by the words I have been inspired to write.

THE BEFORE...

It must have all started with Eve.

After light was given by God to the formless earth and the empty darkness, that faint but welcoming light must have been a beacon and a glimpse of what was to come.

After God's massive canopy appeared above the waters, the beauty of the sky and the awesomeness of the waters became the background of God's palette.

After the waters were gathered together and land began to appear, God's palette exploded with beauty and imagination exposing pristine beaches and pounding surf, snow-capped mountains reaching upward, rolling prairies and open fields, crystal clear lakes with rocky shores, dry and wide deserts, rolling rivers, plants bearing seeds, and trees bearing fruit.

After the sun and the moon and the stars and all those other heavenly creations erupted from God's palette into the far reaches of the universe, the setting was created for the marvelous sunrises and sunsets that gloriously herald each new day and each new evening.

After the stage was set for life, water creatures and birds appeared as whales spouted water in the seas, salmon swam upstream in the river rapids, minnows wiggled in the cold waters of the lakes, eagles soared high in the brilliant blue sky, hummingbirds flitted among the beautiful foliage of the flowers, and geese honked noisily amongst the puffy white clouds. Land creatures appeared as cows lowed in the fertile pastures, beavers built dams in the river rapids, and chimpanzees cavorted through the trees.

God's work was complete and perfect and good.

And then God created man in his own image to live in the midst of his wonderful creation. This man, tenderly created by God's loving hands, was given the best, and God walked beside him to teach him about the creation and how to use it and care for it.

The man did as he was told and all seemed well. However, God's compassion and love allowed him to see that the man was lonely, and it was not good for him to be alone.

So God created Eve.

Eve was created to stand beside Adam—not behind him and not before him—but beside him in equality. She was to share and enjoy all the gifts God had provided for Adam and her. She was to be a complement to Adam as he was to her. Life for Adam and Eve should have been as perfect as the world in which they lived.

The perfection, however, was shattered when Eve, using the free will God had given her and Adam, chose to listen to the serpent. His lies deceived Eve who, in turn, led Adam to disobey God. That's probably when the finger-pointing began and the words of blame and discord filled the air.

And everything changed.

The Bible, we know, is God's Word and was written by man. Most of the narratives place man in the main role with many of the woman taking a lesser role. Did this lesser role begin with Eve? We don't know, but the pattern seems to have been set by her and her actions.

Many women of the Bible were not even given a name. Noah's wife was mentioned only as his wife, but her role had to have been an important one. Noah needed her by his side as a complement in equality.

Other women were not even mentioned even though they had to have been there. The innkeeper's wife surely played a large role on that night in Bethlehem when Jesus was born.

With my writing I have tried to use my imagination to reach into the minds of some of those unnamed and unmentioned women. I have attempted to share their stories of fear, injustice, facing tragedies, sharing their convictions, accepting grace, and receiving God's gift.

As we look into the persona of these woman, we find that each of them had an experience which women of today can use to heal, to grow, and to move forward. It is important to remember how all these women were loved unconditionally by God. Even though their stories do not tell us, we know that God created them all as equal to man. God's master plan was perfect...it was man (and woman) who caused all the problems.

1

NOAH'S WIFE

Changing Fear to Trust
(Genesis 6-9)

Hello. I come to you from long ago and far away. I lived at a time when the world was basically new. Ours was a simple world. We knew little about the greater world as we lived within the confines of our immediate environment. I had always felt mostly content and secure in my surroundings. I obeyed my husband, took care of my family's needs, and adapted to changes as best I could.

However, I would like to share with you a frightening and almost unbelievable event that happened to me and my family so many years ago—an event that changed everything.

The day when this all began was an ordinary day. I was busy in my kitchen preparing a meal for my family. The warm kitchen was filled with the tantalizing smell of the lentil stew I was making, a favorite of my husband, Noah, our three sons, and their wives. I glanced out the window and saw Noah rushing toward our house from the fields. He had an urgent and worried look on his face, and I was curious and a bit frightened. Little did I know that he was bringing news that would shatter life as I knew it.

The world in which we lived had become a terrible place full of violence and was corrupt in God's sight. We had always tried to adapt to worldly changes, but the changes were now more than we could accept. Noah, however, always remained righteous and faithful to God. We had reared our three sons to walk faithfully with God, and each of them had taken a wife who followed our beliefs. Unfortunately it seemed the rest of the world had taken a different path.

Unspeakable acts occurred daily, and I think the violence concerned me most of all. I dreaded my trips to the market for I never knew what might happen on the way there or on the way home. I could sense people looking at me. Sometimes they laughed at me, and I knew it was because of the fear that showed on my face. I also felt they shunned me for the position my family had taken against corruption. I always tried to conceal my fear and to hold my head high. I attended to my needs, avoided eye contact, and returned home as quickly as possible.

When Noah came running into the kitchen that day, he shared the news that he had received a message from God—a message to build an ark because God was going to flood the earth, which would put an end to all people except the ones on that ark. Ark? Flood? I had absolutely no idea what an ark might be and I had no concept of the word flood.

Patiently Noah explained that an ark was a really big boat, which our family would live in for a period of time. I had seen small boats people had used to cross the rivers, but the idea of a boat large enough to hold our entire family? I had no desire to live in a boat for a day much less a longer period of time. The idea seemed impossible to me, not to mention crazy!

And as if that weren't hard enough to understand, Noah then explained that pairs of every living creature, male and female, would be coming to us to seek safety on the ark. All the animals on the boat with us too? Would the animals endanger us? Would they be hostile amongst themselves? All kinds of fears exploded in my mind.

And then came his explanation of the flood—I had never seen water fall from the sky. The earth had always been watered by underground springs, and he was telling me that everything on earth would be covered with water falling from the sky? I tried to imagine that scenario, but I couldn't. It was all beyond my grasp.

I really thought Noah had lost his mind. And he was saying that God had given him this message? The man was crazy! I looked at Noah with fear and disbelief in my eyes and heart. How could any of this happen? I prayed that he would forget this absurd idea of his.

As I tried to process everything Noah told me, I also felt indignation. The very idea that my husband expected me to accept this ridiculous plan of his raised my emotion to an intense level. I longed to yell at him, shake him, ask him how he dared to expect my cooperation! I prayed even harder that this preposterous idea would go away. But I was just a woman with no rights to express my feelings, so I clenched my teeth and waited for my anger to lessen, which it did. The fear and the disbelief, however, remained while I waited for Noah's idea to fade away.

The idea did not go away, but instead became a reality.

The building of the ark began right away. Noah explained that he did not know how long it would take to build the ark before water would begin falling from the sky. This water, which Noah called rain, would begin and continue for forty days and forty nights. Forty days and forty nights living on a boat with all those animals, both tame and wild! I was terrified!

Noah worked with a determination that is impossible to describe. Somehow he convinced our three sons that he had a plan from God, and the four of them worked from sunup until sundown. I still thought they were all crazy, but I managed to keep my thoughts to myself. As a woman, my role was to listen and obey without asking questions. But, oh, the fear and dread I continually experienced!

I was not the only one who thought Noah was crazy. People began coming by to see what was being built. At first they were mostly curious, but when they discovered the purpose of the big boat, the jeering and the ridicule began. It seemed someone was always shouting insults, sometimes alone and sometimes in groups. I stayed mostly in our house except for my infrequent trips to the market where I received jeers and insults as well. I lived in a constant state of distress and disbelief.

My disbelief did not abate during those long years until strange animals eventually began to show up, most of which I had never before seen. What were they? Where did they come from? As time progressed, I began to think that perhaps this flood was really going to happen just as Noah had explained.

When the ark was almost completed, Noah instructed me to begin collecting food and supplies. My sons' wives willingly followed my directions and helped. I caught glimpses of disbelief amongst them. I was sure they questioned my sanity as well. We busied ourselves with collecting food that would sustain our family. What if we ran out of food? What if the food spoiled? Would we starve?

Those years during which they built the ark were the longest and most terrifying I had ever spent. Just the idea that four men could accomplish such a feat was more than my mind could handle. I had many sleepless nights and sometimes lacked appetite or energy. From time to time fear would grip my entire being!

Somehow the ark *was* eventually finished, and with trepidation in my heart, I entered the boat along with the rest of my family. Noah guided all the waiting animals inside, and strangely they all seemed to know what to do and where to go. And then miraculously the door closed and we were all safe inside.

I thought that maybe God had closed the door.

The rain began and as the waters increased, the ark floated high above the ground. Even though I could not see what happened outside, I knew that every other living thing must have perished, and I was deeply saddened. It was all just as my husband had said it would be.

As I began to realize how wrong I had been with my thoughts, I asked God for forgiveness and gave him thanks for my faithful husband. What a great risk he had taken, but he was aware of God's presence all the time! If only I had more trust in God.

As Noah had said, the rain continued for forty days and forty nights and the water flooded the earth for a hundred and fifty days. We did not run out of food...no one got sick...no accidents occurred. Even the animals lived in peaceful harmony. We all experienced a blissful peace and a warm sense of togetherness.

We had to start life all over again after we left the ark. It was not easy, but God protected us and blessed us. He even promised to never destroy the earth with flooding again, and he put a sign in the sky to seal his promise—a beautiful rainbow.

Many years later I looked back on the experience I had feared so much. The whole time God had been faithful and protected us with his loving care. If I had been more trusting, then the journey would have been even more awesome to behold! Afterwards, I still worried about all the death and destruction that had occurred. The world was still not a perfect place, but somewhere in a small place in my heart, I felt that hope was on the way. I didn't know what form the hope would take, but I did believe that God had a plan. I knew he was faithful, and I could feel his great love for his people.

Enough about me. Let's talk about you.

Most of you have experienced that dry-mouth, rapid heart beat feeling that occurs when you are overcome with fear. A dear one dies...an accident happens...a medical emergency occurs...a child is in peril...the list is endless, and no matter how you try to avoid it, fear grips your heart and squeezes it. It's difficult to remember that God is right there with you in your time of need. In fact, sometimes it's difficult to think about God at all. However, if you use the guide God has given you, the Bible, you can learn to find comfort in your time of need.

Remember the disciples crossing the lake when the furious squall came up? It must have been quite a storm because those seasoned fishermen feared they would drown! Upon awaking, Jesus calmed the wind and the waves, and then asked them why they had been afraid. He had been right there with them the whole time!

Isaiah 12:2 tells us, "Surely God is my salvation. I will trust and not be afraid." Trust can be a difficult concept. You may want to trust in God, but with fear squeezing your heart, trust can fly right out the window. Deuteronomy 31:6 tells us, "The Lord himself goes before you and will be with you: he will never leave you nor forsake you. Do not be afraid."

Tragedies come in all sizes, but few, if any, of you have ever seen "the earth give way and the mountains fall into the heart of the sea though its waters roar and foam and the mountains quake with their surging" (Psalm 46:2-3). But you might have seen an unconscious child, a dying mate, the ravages of nature—fire, storms, floods—or a terrible accident. Psalm 46:1 tells you that "God is our refuge and strength, an ever-present help in trouble. Therefore we will not fear."

So the challenge before you is to transform fear into a confident trust. Believe and ask God to help you in your time of need. He will command you to be strong and courageous. He will tell you not to be terrified nor discouraged. He is the Lord your God and will be with you wherever you go.

Usually when the crisis has subsided, you can look back on your experience and wonder why you were so fearful. God was there all the time, loving you and holding you up. God is faithful, and he protects us with his loving care.

Surely God is my salvation. I will trust and not be afraid (Isaiah 12:2).

God was with Noah's wife all the time. Her fear raged and her confidence plummeted, but God stood by her just as he stood by Noah. And even though the rules of that time did not allow her to verbalize her fears and concerns, slowly the experience allowed her to be calm and her confidence to grow. Her fear became trust and she was not afraid.

And just imagine the stories she had to share with her grandchildren...

2

THE PERSISTENT WIDOW

Dealing With Injustice
(Luke 18:1-8)

Hello. I come to you from long ago and far away to share with you my story of being my own advocate in an unjust situation and of my determined persistence to receive justice. Jesus used my story to teach others about mercy and justice.

Throughout history women have played a somewhat inferior role. This seemed especially true during my lifetime! When my husband died, I was left in dire circumstances. We were not wealthy, but we had been able to live comfortably. Life had been good, but now I found myself in trouble. You see, in those days, all the father's inheritance went to the sons, and nothing, yes nothing, went to the widowed wife! To complicate matters even further, my sons had absolutely no interest in providing any care for me. Their selfish lifestyles consumed them, and they welcomed their inheritance with no thoughts of me.

The emotional effect of their indifference toward me was most painful, but I didn't allow myself to be consumed with bitterness. I had to focus on finding a solution to my survival!

At first I was able to eke out a living. I had always enjoyed weaving and was proficient at the loom. I was able to weave some beautiful fabrics, but the cost of the yarn usually negated the profit of selling the fabric. I had even set up a small booth outside my house where I sold objects, both useful and decorative, that I had collected over the years. Some were treasures to me, and I felt pain as I sold them to strangers.

My circumstances did not improve but only worsened. The situation reached the point where my cupboards were almost bare and I was running out of food. As a last resort I planned to seek help from the only person who could perhaps assure me fair treatment—the city judge.

In those days judges traveled around from place to place and held court under a tent. They set their own agenda, and the only way to guarantee an audience with them was to offer a bribe to the attendant of the judge. The attendant would then bring the case before the judge.

Even though I had no money for a bribe, I decided to go forward with my plan, knowing that I would have to be patient, persistent, and persevering.

So there I was, a widow with no money for a bribe, a stranger on my own with no promise of an answer, but not willing to be ignored even though my voice as a woman carried little weight. I prayed to God for help and set out on my mission.

Many judges were corrupt and ruthless, and as luck would have it, I found that described the judge I approached. I desperately needed legal protection to regain a portion of the proceeds my husband and I had accrued during our lifetime together. I was also faced with the fear that my adversaries, my sons, might also approach the judge with a bribe which would render my case useless.

Daily I stood outside the judge's tent, praying for justice. The line of people seeking help from him formed early in the morning and quickly grew long as it moved slowly. Everyone was anxious and tempers were short. Everyone grew hot, tired, and hungry, yet we stood and awaited our turn.

Whenever I had a chance to approach the judge's attendant, I told him, "Grant me justice against my adversary," but when I could produce no bribe, I was sent away. As I approached the attendant daily, the look on the judge's face told me that my actions were getting his attention. I knew that he had heard me, and I prayed that he was listening. Oh, how I prayed!

I tried to think of anything that might entice the judge to hear my plea. Perhaps if I looked different...I tried different hair styles...I wore different garments...I even tore an outfit into tatters hoping he would feel compassionate.

Days came and went. I followed the judge and his tent as he moved from place to place around the city. I prayed continually for justice to prevail. I never lost heart, but I did become oh, so weary.

And then the day I had prayed so hard for finally arrived.

The events happened so quickly that I barely had time to become excited. I was granted an audience with the judge; he listened to my plea and acted positively on it! I wasn't sure if he did so because it was the right thing to do, or because my persistence had worn him down. I thought probably he just wanted me to stop bothering him because his previous actions had shown that he did not respect God and his justice.

As I left the judge's tent that day, my weariness gone, I felt such gratitude to the judge. Regardless of why the judge had acted positively, I felt that I would be eternally grateful to him.

As I approached the door to my house, which I would now be able to maintain and enjoy, I suddenly had a huge revelation—I had mistaken the source of my help. How could my thinking have been so wrong? If an unjust judge listens, how much more quickly will God listen! I had prayed continually, I had been patient, I had been persistent, and I had persevered all because God had been beside me through the entire process. My gratitude belonged to God—he was my advocate!

From that day forward, I continued to thank God for his goodness and for being by my side. I shared my experience with others and encouraged them to be persistent in their endeavors. I wanted everyone to know that mercy and justice could be obtained with prayer and faith in our heavenly Father.

And now you...

If ever you must deal with an injustice in your life, give thought to the persistent widow's story and give thanks that your circumstances are surely less than hers. Whatever the circumstances, stand firm in your belief and never lose heart. Pray without ceasing, and ask God, your advocate, for help and guidance. Remember that you can come boldly to God who is your righteous Father. He has promised you that he will never forsake you. Access to God is unlimited. You don't have to wait outside a tent or offer a bribe; you can pray to him at anytime and anywhere, and he will listen. If expressing the injustice is difficult, your prayer doesn't need to be eloquent or laden with specific requests. Even before you try to explain, God is aware of your plea. Just give your circumstances to God and rest in his love. And God, because he is your heavenly Father, is delighted when you ask for his help!

If God is for us, who can be against us? (Romans 8:31b)

It's such a comfort to know that God is in our corner. We know we can approach him at any time through our prayers, and we must remember to thank him for his presence. We go to him with the big problems, but sometimes we forget to go to him with the little ones. If we remember to be thankful for all things, it seems only right to know that he will take care of them—big and small.

3

JEPHTHAH'S DAUGHTER

Facing Tomorrow
(Judges 11:29-40)

Hello. I am the daughter of Jephthah, and I come to you from long ago and far away to share the story of a portion of my life with you. It's a sad story and does not have a happy ending.

My father, Jephthah, a Gileadite, was a mighty warrior. I was his only child. I loved my father dearly, and he loved me. I was the apple of his eye. In our home in Mizpah, I had grown up listening to the stories of his great battles and victories. His triumphs were known far and near. I was so very proud of him. For as long as I could remember, I always anxiously awaited his return from battle. When I ran out to meet him, he would grab me into his muscular arms and hold me tightly.

My life was idyllic. I had no worries—all my whims were catered to, and I had grown into a beautiful young woman, or so my father said. I had heard whisperings that several young men in our village had taken notice of me. My friends and I giggled about that, but at the same time it was indeed flattering. And so I was living a blissful life of contentment and joy.

On the day when my life changed, I had spent a wonderful morning in the meadows picking wild flowers. The meadow was filled with field after field of color—pinks, yellows, and purples. I had used the beautiful flowers to make a crown for my head and bracelets for my wrists and ankles. I had lain on my back in the midst of the beauty and aroma of the flowers and enjoyed the sensation of the world around me. I had taken my tambourine with me for I loved to dance, and the best place to dance was the beautiful outdoor surroundings. So I danced and sang and laughed and enjoyed the pleasure of just being alive.

Lunch hour was approaching, and the activities of the morning had given me a healthy appetite. I gathered the beautiful flowers I had picked to give to my mother for a bouquet, and holding them in my arms along with my tambourine, started down the grassy hill toward our home.

I was shaking my tambourine and dancing all the way home. I found a vase for the flowers and was placing them on the table when I heard the noise of my father returning from his most recent battle. His returns created excitement, and we always celebrated with food and dancing as we listened to the stories of his exploits and victories. I grabbed my tambourine and danced out to greet him.

When my father saw me coming, I expected to see a smile on his face and open arms to hold me. Instead I saw first a look of disbelief and then a look of absolute anguish. He began flailing his arms, tearing his clothes, crying, and yelling. I was frightened, and I didn't understand. My father was always so kind and gentle with me. I could understand only parts of what he was saying, something about how I had made him miserable and wretched, and how he had made a vow to the Lord that he could not break. I couldn't understand! His tirade continued for some time while I stood before him, shaking with fear and crying uncontrollably.

When he finally calmed down, he took me in his arms and soothed my fears and wiped away my tears. It seemed that perhaps everything was going to be fine, but then I learned the cause of his distress. Yes, he had returned victorious from his latest battle, but it seemed the victory was due to a deal he had made with God. He had made a vow that if the Lord would give the enemy, the Ammonites, into his hands, he would offer as a burnt offering whatever came out of his house to greet him when he returned victorious. And who had danced out to meet him—I had!

Most certainly when my father made this vow with God, he had pictured a household pet or a courtyard animal running to meet him. He could not have pictured his only child, his beloved daughter, being sacrificed as a burnt offering. I was nevertheless horrified! However I knew he was a man of his word, and that he must and would do as he had promised God. What I didn't understand was why he had even considered making this vow. He knew that God was with him—his victories were proof of that! Why had he not relied on God's faithfulness?

As I processed what was to happen to me, I was overcome with grief. It occurred to me that I would never marry, never give birth to a child, an heir, and I probably would be forgotten as time went on. I needed some time to absorb all of this!

As many thoughts rushed through my mind, I suddenly felt the need for the companionship of my peers. I had many friends. I loved them and they loved me, and they could comfort me and be by side during this ordeal.

I stepped away from my father's embrace and asked him to grant me one request, "Give me two months to roam the hills and weep with my friends, because I will never marry" (Judges 11:37).

He granted my request.

Quickly my friends and I gathered food and supplies and headed for the hills, the beautiful hills where I had danced and picked so many lovely flowers. We were a solemn group for we knew the doom that was looming in the near future for me. The first few days we did little but cry and lament. How could this be? It wasn't fair! My life was to be cut short without a husband and children! I would be forgotten in the future. My short life would be meaningless!

One morning we all came to the realization that we could do nothing to fix my circumstances and decided to change our focus. Slowly we began to relax and reflect on happy memories. We began singing and dancing and enjoying our beautiful surroundings. We thanked God for all his blessings, especially the blessing of our friendship. We felt God's presence and rested in his peace.

We were young and we created fantasies of what our lives could have been in the future. We imagined handsome husbands, beautiful children, and lovely homes where we could entertain one another. My healing began with the help of my amazing friends and the presence of God's love.

The days flew by and the two months were soon over. As

we gathered our belongings and headed down the hill to my parent's house, I felt as if a balm had been poured over my body. I could face tomorrow because of the love bestowed on me by my friends and by God.

After two months, she returned to her father and he did to her as he had vowed (Judges 11:39).

Jephthah's daughter was not forgotten as her death created an Israelite custom. Every year the young women of Israel would go out by themselves for four days to remember the life of the daughter of Jephthah the Gileadite. And we too remember her even today.

And now you. . .

None of you will ever have to face the possibility of being sacrificed as a burnt offering, but a time may come when you will have to "face tomorrow." That tomorrow might hold the death of a loved one, a divorce, a financial ruin, or a bad diagnosis from a doctor. If you should be faced with a heart-stopping situation, know that it's normal to be horrified. It's normal to question. It's normal to be angry. But when reality sets in and you are ready to change your focus, try to wrap your mind around the fact that you are not alone. Go to your cadre of friends, share with them, let them hold you in their arms and cry with you. Go to your church family, share with your pastors, ask for a Stephen minister. If you feel the need, seek professional help. Talk with others and openly express your feelings to all who care.

When you've done all that you can do and still feel despair, there is one more place to go—sit at Jesus' feet and tell him all about it. Cry with him. Let him hold you in his arms and give you peace. Knowing that all situations do not end as we would like them to, rest assured that Jesus will see you through your difficulties and will be with you to the end.

And surely I am with you always, to the very end of the age (Matthew 28:20).

The sad story of Jephthah's daughter is difficult to comprehend. In today's world we cannot stretch our imagination enough to even consider such a thing happening. However, bad things do happen all the time. Daily the media report of atrocities full of hate and violence happening to innocent victims. And often when reality sets in, it becomes evident that nothing can change what has happened. In the midst of it all, we must all remain firm in our faith and be confident of God's presence. He is always there and will be by our side until the end.

And let's hope that when those who are faced with atrocities go to meet their fate, they can go with flowers in their arms, shaking their tambourine, and dancing.

4

THE ISRAELITE MIDWIFE

Making a Difference
(Exodus 1:15-22)

Hello. I am a young Israelite girl. I come to you from long ago and far away to share with you some decisions I helped to make. One of those decisions played an extremely important part in the lives of the people of Israel.

I lived in the country of Egypt, which was ruled by Pharaoh. The region in which I lived was the delta of the Nile River. The land was beautiful and abundant.

My childhood had been a happy one even though my family lived in bondage. My father did hard labor with brick and mortar. I knew life was bitter, but my mother did all she could to protect me. And because her protection shielded me, I knew little of the trials of the world in which we lived.

But the day arrived when I needed to plan for my future. It was time to be an adult. I had always felt compelled to help others, especially the ill and infirm. But probably more than that, I loved babies and hoped to someday have some of my own.

My mother had two friends, Shiphrah and Puah, who were midwives in the service of Pharaoh. They were in charge of the corps of midwives, and I had heard many stories of how they had helped women bring their beautiful babies into the world. Even though some of the birthing experiences were unpleasant, it was the precious babies who captured my attention. And so, I decided that I too would like to become a midwife.

With my mother by my side, I approached Shiphrah and Puah who both agreed that I could come into service with them. I was elated!

After several weeks of observation, my first real responsibility was to clean the babies after they were born and to wrap them in warm clothes. Oh, how precious they were, and I loved cuddling them in my arms and comforting them with soft whispers!

One day as I was singing softly to a beautiful baby boy in my arms, a messenger came to tell us that Pharaoh himself was on his way to our quarters. We panicked! What could Pharaoh possibly want from us? He had never approached us before. I had only seen him from afar, and now I was to stand in his presence. I was terrified.

We quickly straightened our quarters and ourselves, and then waited, almost at attention, for him to enter.

With much fanfare, Pharaoh and his entourage stormed into our quarters. In a loud, harsh voice, he announced that beginning right that moment any baby boy delivered to a slave woman, an Israelite, should be put to death, but girl babies could live.

I was appalled! The boy babies were to die? How could this happen? My mind went into a tailspin. I remembered hearing Pharaoh was distressed that the Israelites, whom he held in bondage, had become too numerous, and there were many more Israelites than Egyptians. Pharaoh had worked the Israelite men relentlessly, but still they continued to multiply. Could it be that he was frightened that he might lose his power and be overthrown as king of Egypt if they became too numerous? That must have been the reason! But to kill babies?

Pharaoh left as abruptly as he had entered. Dead silence filled our quarters. And then Shiphrah began to cry and crumbled to the floor. Puah's ashen face was full of disbelief. And I...I could hardly move, much less speak. We were drawn into one another's arms and stood in a circle of embrace.

And then it was as if God had spoken to us, and a plan formed in our minds. We could possibly continue our role as midwives and tell Pharaoh that the slave women were not like the Egyptians—they were strong and vigorous and gave birth before we could help them. (After all men, even Pharaoh, didn't know much about the birthing process!).

We talked it over carefully. We knew the dangers of our plan and we knew what could happen if we failed. If we were to enact our plan, we had to be strong and courageous.

The plan was scary and dangerous, but our decision was that God would want us to follow through with it. The boy babies must live! We could not let them die.

Our plan worked for quite a while. Bravely we continued our daily routine as usual, and we began to feel that perhaps all would be well. Perhaps Pharaoh's attention had moved on to other matters such as building monuments and amassing wealth. However, the day arrived that we probably had been

25

expecting in the recesses of our mind. It seemed that Pharaoh had noticed that the Israelites were still increasing in number, and he summoned us for an explanation.

We rehearsed what we would say and felt confident because we knew that God was on our side. We were strong and faced Pharaoh without fear. We bravely explained how strong and vigorous the slave women were and how they gave birth without our assistance. He must have believed us. Otherwise I fear we would have been put to death.

One good part of my story is that we didn't have to kill any boy babies. The bad part is that later Pharaoh issued a new decree that every baby boy who was born must be thrown into the Nile River. The best part of my story is that during our time of disobedience to Pharaoh, many Israelite baby boys were born and were allowed to live. Even after Pharaoh's decree, many baby boys were spared the death of drowning, and one of them was named Moses.

And now you. . .

Civil disobedience requires a person to be strong and courageous. Fear must be overcome and discouragement cannot be present. The young midwife faced Pharaoh and refused to be a part in the murder of innocent babies much as Rosa Parks faced adversity by refusing to sit in the back of the bus. In your life you may never be faced with such a dramatic decision, but in the wrongs of our world, it's important to take a stand and speak against hurt, pain, and injustice. Mobs yelling and screaming and riots are definitely not the answer, while kind acts may be. If you and I treat others as we wish to be treated, if we speak with kindness, if we share with those less fortunate than ourselves, and if we lead the life that

God would have us live, we can make a difference. The difference might be small, but perhaps could grow into something big as other join us.

Be strong and courageous. Do not be afraid or discouraged (Chronicles 22:13).

Micah 6:8 tells us what the Lord requires of us: "to act justly, love mercy, and walk humbly with your God." That seems to say it all.

5

PILATE'S WIFE

Standing Up for Your Beliefs
(Matthew 27:19)

Hello. I am the wife of Pilate, the Roman governor of Judea. I come to you from long ago and far away to tell you about the time I tried to implore my husband not to make a wrong decision. It took much courage to speak up to the governor of Judea even though he was my husband, but I felt compelled to do so because of a dream I had.

We had just arrived in Jerusalem for the Feast of the Passover. Our home was a palace in Caesarea Philippi near the Sea of Galilee where I lived a contented life. However, I loved to come to Herod's palace in Jerusalem because it was so luxurious.

We hosted wonderful parties with banquet tables seating scores of important guests. Everything was opulent with gold serving pieces and finely crafted cutlery and utensils. Sumptuous meals were prepared for our guests and only the best wine was served.

I especially loved the colonnades with mosaic tiles and

marble columns. From there I could enjoy the beautiful gardens abundant with all sorts of exotic flowers. The beauty and fragrance almost took my breath away.

From the side of a colonnade, I first saw the man Jesus. He was surrounded by crowds of people who seemed to adore him. He always appeared to be calm and caring and very tender. I had heard from many people about his ministry and the miracles he had performed.

I knew about his turning water into wine at a wedding in Cana in Galilee.

I knew about the time he crossed to the far shore of the Sea of Galilee and throngs of people followed him—some said as many as five thousand. I had heard how he had taken five small barley loaves and two small fish from a young boy, given thanks for the food, and given it to his disciples to distribute amongst the hungry crowd. It was said that everyone was fed and much was left over!

I had heard about the healing of men with leprosy, the deliverance of the demon-possessed men, the curing of paralytics, and even the healing of his disciple Peter's mother-in-law, and the raising from the dead of his friend Lazarus.

I was indeed intrigued.

Even though I was a Roman and he was Jewish, I recognized good when I saw it. Something in my heart told me this was no ordinary man, and I desired to learn more about him and perhaps even become a follower.

It was not to be.

Upon arising one morning I sensed tension and unrest amongst our servants. When I inquired as to what was happening, a slave girl informed me that the man Jesus had been arrested the previous night. The chief priests and elders, led by the high priest Caiaphas, had plotted against Jesus and planned to kill him. When I asked why they wanted to kill him, she explained it was because he claimed to be King of the Jews. As I pondered this over in my mind, I reasoned that the chief priests and elders were threatened and scared of this claim.

But how could something like this happen to this kind, loving man who had done no wrong? He had led no rebellions! He had just sat day by day in the temple courtyards teaching and explaining the laws of his God. He had performed so many wonderful miracles that had changed so many lives. This simply could not happen, but what could I do?

I went to my bed chambers to prepare myself for the day. My slave irritated me while braiding my hair, and I rudely sent her away. The clothing she had chosen for me landed in a heap on the floor. I scattered my jewelry on the floor and didn't bother to pick it up. Nothing seemed right—I felt exhausted and experienced the beginning of a headache. I glanced at my rumpled bed, closed the curtains around it to keep out the light, crawled in, and promptly fell asleep.

Awakening some time later, it took me an inordinate time to focus my thoughts. I had had the most astonishing dream, and my whole being was absorbed with bewilderment. I had dreamed about the man Jesus. I had seen his acts of kindness and felt his loving presence. His short life flashed through my mind, beginning with his humble birth and ending with last night's arrest. I had seen the hurt in his follower's eyes. I had felt the pain in the precious heart of his mother. And my entire being ached with compassion. This was no ordinary man, and I felt that my dream must surely be a message from a higher being.

I had to do something and I had to do it quickly!

I knew that court was now in session. I knew that a decision was near at hand. I also knew of the custom to release a prisoner during the Feast of the Passover and that the released prisoner was always chosen by the crowd. I also knew of another prisoner, the notorious Barabbas, who was imprisoned for an act of insurrection and for murder.

I had to act and act quickly.

I would have loved to have made my way to the courtroom and to have begged for the dismissal of the charges against Jesus, but the guards would have barred my entrance. After all I was only a woman even though my husband was the governor. So I did the only thing I could think of. I quickly scribbled a note to my husband, urging him to have nothing to do with Jesus and even giving him a few details of my dream. Taking the note I ran out into the palace courtyard where I found a young slave boy watering the flowers. Giving him the note, I instructed him to run as fast as he could and deliver the message to no one but Pilate.

And then I waited.

Returning to my bed chambers, I tried to keep busy. I called for my slave to come braid my hair. We even tried some new styles. My slave drew my warm, scented bath and while I enjoyed the comforting warmth, she carefully chose my gown and jewelry for that night's dinner.

I could hear sounds coming from the street, but I didn't dare go to the colonnade to observe. I was afraid of what I might see.

Shortly after the midday hour, I heard the slaves scurrying around as they always did when Pilate entered the palace. I heard him approach my chambers and open the door. I turned to look at him, saying nothing. He sat down on the edge of my bed, held his head in his hands and said, "They chose Barabbas."

And now you. . .

Perhaps the time will come in your life when you just have to stand up and say your piece. When you care for others in the name of Jesus Christ, speaking up may be challenging, complicated, and even discouraging. But if you shield yourself with the fruit of the Spirit—love, joy, peace, patience, kindness, goodness, faithfulness, and self-control—you can at least set a Christ-like example. And then, regardless of the end result of your speaking up, you can rest assured that you have acted as the Spirit has led you.

Pray so that the Lord will give me the confidence to say what I have to say (Ephesians 6:20b).

So put on your armor, let the Spirit lead you and say what you feel God has led you to say. You are sure to feel an inner peace afterwards.

6

THE SAMARITAN WOMAN

Accepting the Gift of Grace
(John 4:1-26)

Hello. I am a woman of Samaria, and I come to you from long ago and far away to share the story of how the man Jesus came into my life. What happened to me is precious and amazing. And perhaps the best part is that what happened to me can happen to anyone! I hope my story will be a reminder that anyone can be forgiven of their sins.

The story of my life is not pleasant and is difficult for me to share. I lived in the town of Sychar, between Jerusalem and Nazareth, in Samaria. The man I lived with owned property near Jacob's well. This was a communal well on the ground Jacob had given to his son Joseph so many years ago. Many of the women of the town visited the well twice daily, once in the cool of the morning and then in the shade of the evening, to draw water for use in their homes.

I *never* visited the well at those times for I was considered to be an outcast by all who knew me or knew of me. I had been married five times prior to living with my current lover, and I knew the gossipy women would shame me. I had no friends and I did not know any of the women, but they certainly knew all about me. I felt that probably I was the topic of conversation at many of their gatherings. The well was also a gathering place for the women to share idle gossip, and I did not want to put myself in a position to be scorned.

I knew my loose way of living was wrong. After my first marriage failed, I seemed to no longer care about myself or my pride. My face had once been pretty but now was hard. My once beautiful hair was now tangled and matted for I gave little attention to personal care. My tired body gave no hint to my previous girlish figure. I once found pleasure in stylish clothes and jewelry, but now I found myself in tattered, and most often, soiled clothing. I moved from day to day in a fog of unhappiness and had reached the point of thinking my life had no hope of changing or improving.

I merely existed.

On the day I met the man Jesus, I had gone to the well in the heat of the day. The midday sun scorched the earth, and I could feel the heat through my thin sandals. My flimsy headdress did little to keep me cool, and perspiration ran down my face from the strain of carrying the heavy water jars. And yet, I felt secure in the knowledge that I would encounter no one. However, as I approached the well, I was surprised to see a man resting against the side of the well.

Samaria was the shortest route between Judea and Galilee, and even though we Samaritans were considered to be outsiders, many people, including Jews, chose to use this route for traveling between areas. Probably the main reason for our being considered as outsiders was the fact that we did not consider Jerusalem as the center of our religion—we claimed Mt. Gerizim as our center. It didn't seem to me that a location would make such a difference, but it did. Travelers passing through our area avoided making eye contact with us and never did we speak to one another, much less offer assistance or show any form of acceptance. When I saw the strange man resting against Jacob's well, I was shocked and concerned. Should I ignore him or turn and go home?

But then he spoke to me...

The idea that he had spoken to me was unbelievable! Ours was a patriarchal society, and all women were thought to be inferior to men. And men did not speak to women in public, not even to their wife, mother, or sister. As women we were expected to take care of our families and our homes. Beyond that we had no role at all. I stood there stunned!

And then I realized he had asked me for a drink of water.

I could tell by his accent and his clothing that he was a Jew. Jews hated Samaritans! Any drink that I might hand him would be considered unclean, not because of my loose way of living, but simply because I was a Samaritan. Knowing this, I summoned the courage to ask him how he could even consider asking me, a Samaritan, for water.

The conversation that followed forever changed my life. Speaking in symbolic language and using water as an example, he explained to me about living water and everlasting life. He knew *all* my secrets, and my lurid way of life. Yet he saw worth in me for he shared the plan of salvation with me. Me! A sinful Samaritan woman!

As I processed all that he had told me, I instantly felt an

overwhelming cleansing and realized that I was talking not to an ordinary man but to the Messiah. I didn't understand how all this happened, but my ears seemed to open and my eyes seemed to see and I just knew!

Just then a few men arrived at the well with baskets of food. I could tell they viewed me in a negative manner—as a woman, as a Samaritan, and as a sinner. Giving me scornful looks, they asked Jesus why he was even talking to me. Whereas their comments would have shamed me in the past, I felt no rebuke. Leaving my water jars by the well, I hurried back to Sychar. I had some good news that I could hardly wait to share—the good news that anyone can be forgiven of their sins.

(Upon the Samaritan woman's arrival in Sychar, many people chose to listen to her. Evidently they witnessed an amazing change in her for they, too, went to Jacob's well. They begged Jesus to stay, and he remained for two days. Many became believers.)

Many years later when I was an old woman, I often returned to Jacob's well. Sometimes I went there in the cool of the morning and sometimes in the shade of the evening. My clothing, while not luxurious, was clean and presentable. My now white hair shone like a crown upon my head. I held my head high and kept my shoulders straight. I looked at everyone at the well directly in the eye and I felt no scorn. We even smiled and greeted one another.

I continued to share my story of the gift of grace that Jesus had given me. And I felt humbled in knowing that many had listened to me and had received the precious gift as well.

And now you...

What a wonderful gift you've been given—the gift of grace. It does not matter if you've lived a life of near perfection or a life of shame. The living waters of everlasting life and salvation are yours for the taking! It's so simple—just come to Jesus with your sins and burdens and he will give you peace. And you don't have to do a single thing to earn this peace...simply believe!

Come to me, all you who are weary and burdened, and I will give you rest (Matthew 11:28).

Thankfully no mess is too big for God to clean up and renew. Just think of all the times in history when he has intervened and made things right. And then think of all the times he has intervened and made things right that we do not know about—perhaps even with you and me!

7

THE BAHURIM WOMAN

Telling the Truth
(2 Samuel 17:17-22)

Hello. I come to you from long ago and far away during the reign of King David of Israel. I lived in the small village of Bahurim near Jerusalem on the road to the Jordan Valley and on the eastern slope of the Mount of Olives. What I would like to share with you happened in the courtyard of the house that belonged to my husband and me.

I absolutely adored King David. I definitely knew that he was not perfect, but, to me, his faults were overshadowed by his loving heart and his dedication to God. I listened to every snippet I heard about him and pondered all that information in my heart. Whenever he and members of his court or his warriors passed through our small village, I was always at the side of the road to cheer for him. And, oh my yes, he was very handsome too!

I heard that Absalom, David's son, had conspired against his father. He planned to overtake David, ruin him (or even kill him), and attack Jerusalem. How could a son even con-

sider such a thing? I was upset with the very idea! How could
it be?

One morning as I was gazing out my window at the
Mount of Olives, my husband rushed into the house in an
agitated state. It seemed he had heard that two of the king's
messengers were approaching our village on their way to
Jerusalem with information about Absalom's intentions. They
were traveling on foot and Absalom's men were in close pur-
suit. My husband and I knew that we had to act. We needed
to do everything in our power to protect our king and perhaps even aid in saving his life. We came up with a workable
plan and prayed that we would be successful.

My husband hurried to the roadside and when he saw the
messengers approach, he guided them into our courtyard. We
wanted to protect them from the danger of what might occur
if Absalom's men caught them. A dry well stood in the
middle of the courtyard and seemed to be a good hiding
place—perhaps the only hiding place. After explaining the
perilous situation to the men, my husband helped them climb
down into it.

I quickly ran into the house and grabbed a large piece of
cloth with which I had planned to make into a robe for my
husband. I took the cloth outside and spread it over the well
opening. The cloth draped just enough over the side that it
didn't seem too conspicuous. I had gathered stalks of grain
from our garden earlier that morning, and I spread the grain
on top of the cloth. It appeared to be drying in the sun.
Would this fool Absalom's men? I prayed so!

As we saw the dust of pursuers in the distance, my husband returned to the fields where he had been working. I
stayed in the courtyard picking up the bits of grain that had

fallen to the ground. I prayed that our actions would appear normal as part of our regular day.

I heard the men approaching and my heart began to pound in my chest. What would happen?

As the men came into the courtyard, they asked if I had seen two strangers in the area that morning. With a calmness I didn't know I possessed, I told them two men had passed by and crossed over the bridge.

The men left immediately. I could see them searching everywhere near and around the bridge. At some point they must have given up because they finally left. I breathed a sigh of relief and thankfulness.

After what seemed a safe period of time, my husband returned from the fields and helped the messengers out of the well. They were able to continue onward and give King David the warning that possibly could have protected his life and saved Jerusalem from attack.

Later I anguished over the fact that I had told an untruth to Absalom's men. I was human and I made mistakes, but I knew right from wrong. And being untruthful was wrong. After much consideration and prayer, I finally found peace. I felt forgiveness from God because my actions had perhaps kept my king alive. David would never know what I done, but I felt comfort in knowing that I had aided my beloved king. I also felt God's forgiveness in my heart as my intentions were meant to offer protection to David, his men, and Jerusalem.

Later I heard that Absalom's plan failed. David, his men, and Jerusalem were safe for the time being. I often thought of the part I had played in aiding David, and my thoughts put a smile of contentment on my face.

And now you...

You, like the woman of Bahurim, have probably anguished over not having told the truth on some occasion. The "truth" is such a broad topic, ranging from telling a friend her recipe was delicious when you could barely choke it down to making a false statement that could endanger the life or safety of someone.

Mostly you are faced with the little white lie dilemma. Is it wrong to lie about something insignificant rather than to hurt someone's feelings? Is it wrong to lie about an incident rather than to open a whole can of worms and to cause a heated situation? Is it wrong to lie about your status, your possessions, your life in general in the hopes of raising someone's opinion of you? The little white lie list seems to be endless.

Forgiveness awaits you when you lie and are deceitful. The Old Testament presented a strict code of conduct concerning lies and deceit (Leviticus 6:3-7). Thankfully, because of Christ, we live in grace and receive the gift of redemption. Consider Peter who lied three times in his denial of Jesus, and yet he was forgiven and became the rock upon which Christ built the church. The love of Jesus was much stronger than Peter's lies! That love is there for you too.

This little white lie dilemma seems to be a personal battle. Being human you probably will err and/or consider doing so. Let your conscience be your guide. Whatever you choose to do, do it in the love of God and others. And knowing that you will err, ask your God for forgiveness and guidance. And thank him for his unconditional love and grace.

For all have sinned and fall short of the glory of God, and all are justified freely by his grace through the redemption that came by Christ Jesus (Romans 3:23).

Thanks be to God. We are forgiven!

8

THE WIDOW OF ZAREPHATH

Holding On to Your Trust
(1 Kings 17:7-24)

Hello. I am a poor widow and I come to you from long ago and far away to share two happenings in my life, both of which started tragically but ended miraculously. All of my story happened during the reign of Ahab, King of Israel, who was as evil as a man can be.

God was very displeased with Ahab, his followers, and their sinful ways, and he had decided to act upon their disobedience. The action God took was that neither dew nor rain would be present for the next few years. Just take a minute and consider that!

A terrible drought fell upon the land of Israel. Day by day, week by week, month by month, the earth continued to dry up. Crops wilted in the field and died. Planting seeds was futile. Cattle died. Brooks, streams, and wells began to dry up. It was not only a time of drought but was also the beginning of a time of starvation.

I lived in the small town of Zarephath with my young

son. Since the death of my husband, life had been difficult. I had been very frugal. I had kept a small garden of vegetables, herbs, and a few olive trees, which had helped sustain the two of us. And even though it had been difficult, I had maintained a small field of barley. We had been able to survive on our meager lot and even at times had been able to share a small bit with others.

But now I was at my wit's end. The day had come when my food supply was depleted. I had just enough flour and oil to make a small cake of barley bread for my son and me. I was also aware that the brook where we got our water would soon be dry.

Not willing to face defeat, I headed to the fields, walking slowly so as not to exert myself, and gathered twigs to build a fire in my oven. Even the twigs were parched and brittle.

As I was bundling them up, I saw Elijah the prophet approaching me. Even though I knew who he was, I was sure he didn't know me. I had heard that he was a man of God, but my pagan beliefs had no understanding of this God of his. Yet I still had room in my heart to respect his goodness.

As he came near, I could see that he was tired and hot, so it came as no surprise when he asked me for a drink of water. I turned to go to my house for a water jug when he added an impossible request. Would I please bring him a piece of bread as well!

(The widow did not know that God had told Elijah to go to Zarephath and stay there. God also had told Elijah that he had commanded a widow there to supply him with food. Jeremiah 29:11 tells us, "For I know the plans I have for you, plans to prosper you and not to harm you. Plans to give you hope and a future.")

Well, the water I could spare, but the bread? My son needed the bread and so did I. And I knew that most probably the bread I was going to make would be our last meal. Could I possibly share our last meal with this man who was a stranger to me? I tried to kindly explain all this to Elijah, and my jaw dropped at his reply.

He told me to have no fear...no fear? I lived my life in fear—fear of not being able to provide for my child and fear of starvation.

And then he added the really unbelievable part...

He told me that after I made a small cake of bread for him and then some for my son and me, my jar of flour would not be used up and my jug of oil would not run dry until the day his God gave back rain to the land! My mind longed to deny his words, but my heart encouraged me to trust and have faith.

And so I turned, went to my house, and did as Elijah had told me. My hands were shaking as I mixed the flour and oil, just enough for one small cake for Elijah. They shook as I patted out the one small cake, and then miraculously enough dough remained to make another small cake for my son and me! My hands shook as I lit the fire. They shook the whole time the bread was baking. The aroma of the bread made my mouth water.

My son, standing beside me, licked his lips in anticipation! Finally the two browned cakes were ready to eat. I wrapped them in a cloth and took them outside to share with Elijah. How good the bread tasted! We savored each morsel. But in the recesses of my mind, I was still wondering if this would be our last meal.

The sun was hot that day, so I invited Elijah to come inside our house to rest and cool off. He had told me that he was on his way to the wilderness to escape the wrath of Ahab. My heart went out to him. I had a spare upper room and when I offered for him to use it as a refuge, he gladly accepted.

Later, not being able to contain my curiosity and anxiety, I went to my kitchen. I was amazed and relieved to find my flour jar full and my oil jug overflowing! From that day on, my supply of flour and oil never diminished. I thankfully realized that this God of Elijah's would provide. How blessed I was! I began to believe that his God could be my God too, and I experienced an inner calmness beyond description.

This truly had been a miracle and my faith grew strong. Elijah's presence was a constant reminder of God's goodness. But then something happened to shatter my faith and my trust in God disappeared.

I was awakened one night by the cries of my son. As I lifted him from his bed, I could feel the heat coming from his listless body. I began to bathe him with cool cloths, but nothing I did seemed to work. I sat on the floor and cradled him in my arms for the rest of the night. He grew worse and worse, until I just sat there on the floor kissing his lifeless body.

With the approach of morning, Elijah came into the room, and I began yelling at him and blaming him and blaming God. He calmly took my son in his arms and went to his upper room. I was too upset to follow and I continued sitting on the floor and wailing.

A very short time later Elijah returned to me with my son—my son who was alive and well! I didn't know what went on in that upper room, but I knew that God had to have been there. And I knew that Elijah was truly a man of God. His presence and his faith had led me through two tragedies. How humble I felt and how very thankful I was. From that day forward my faith continued to grow. Life was never easy—I was still poor and I was still a widow. But now I had God with me and I could face any possibility.

And now you. . .

In today's world, unfortunately, some people must exist on insufficient food and water or on scraps wherever they may be found. Mothers still hold their dying children in their arms in hopeless agony—you've seen the pictures and heard the news reports. You will also be faced with trials but probably not of the magnitude of the widow of Zarephath, but still trials that will seem paramount to you.

The widow's story is about sharing what we have, and further, trusting, losing that trust, and then regaining it. You know about sharing through the daily reminders that come to you via mail, phone, and media—reminders of the needs of others—and you respond. Food pantries seek assistance in the form of donations, and you respond. Your church offers opportunities to contribute to charities both near and far, and you respond. And there are always random acts of kindness to which you respond.

But responding to trust is not as easy as collecting cans of beans or making a monetary donation. Trust comes from within and grows as your dependence on your heavenly Father grows. Holding on to your trust can be challenged by events in your life that seem like more than you can bear.

And if you do find yourself at the edge of an abyss, always re-member that God is there to keep you from falling or to pull you out. His unconditional love will forgive you for your weakness in not relying on your faith. He will hold you, his child, in his loving arms and restore your faith. Whatever caused your lack of faith may or may not go away, but God will provide a way so that you can stand up under it. Rely on your God and let him hold your hand.

But with God all things are possible (Matthew 19:26b).

And when you rely on your God and let him hold your hand, know that you can face all possibilities.

9

DAVID'S MOTHER

Letting Someone Go
(1 Samuel 16)

Hello. I come to you from long ago and far away. I would like to share with you a heartbreaking event that happened in my life so many years ago.

One morning I looked out my door and saw Samuel the prophet and a group of men approaching our house. I knew Samuel because our town of Bethlehem was small and everybody knew everybody. I thought the men with him were elders because they accompanied him quite often. I had heard some of the elders of the town talking about Samuel and his grief that Saul, who was king over our country of Israel, had ever been anointed as king. I was puzzled as to why Samuel had come to our house, but I went out to greet him.

It seemed Samuel needed to know where Jesse, my husband, and our eight sons were. I directed him to the field where they were tending the sheep. The entourage passed by me, dragging a heifer behind them. I was more puzzled than ever, so I followed behind them as discretely as I could. After all, I was a woman and had no right interfering in the business of men.

When they located my family, Samuel set up an altar and offered the heifer as a sacrifice to the Lord. And then Samuel made an announcement that I knew would impact my life forever. He announced that the Lord had sent him to anoint one of our eight sons as the new king! What? Why us? We were just happy shepherds living an uncomplicated life. How could this happen to us?

One by one our sons passed in front of Samuel. He immediately favored Eliab who was tall and handsome. However the Lord told Samuel that "man looks at the outward appearance but he, the Lord, looks at the heart" (1 Samuel 16:7). And so Eliab was passed over as were the rest of our sons. Realizing he had only seen seven of our sons, Samuel asked about our eighth. David, our youngest who was tending sheep in a distant field, was called to come in from the fields.

I have always remembered David with a lamb in his arms, his face ruddy, his freckles shining on his nose, his hair windblown, running across the fields. He was my baby boy and I treasured him over all our elder sons. My plans were to love him, cherish him, protect him, and keep him close to me.

But my plans were not to be.

Apparently Samuel immediately recognized that David was the chosen one for he took his horn of oil and anointed him in the presence of our family. I fell to my knees and wept. Part of my heart felt pride that God had chosen my boy to be our king, but a bigger part of my heart felt shredded to pieces. He would never belong to his mother again. I felt that he had been ripped from my arms and would never return to the warm embrace we both had shared.

I feared that David would be taken from me that very moment, but that did not happen. He stayed with our family and continued tending the sheep. He grew big, handsome, strong, and took on the responsibility of becoming a great warrior.

But he also had a tender heart and became proficient at playing the harp. Many evenings when chores were finished, I would sit by his side and be soothed by the beautiful music he played on his harp. I knew those moments were precious and would not last.

Just as I feared, the time came when David was summoned by King Saul. Saul, who was tormented by an evil spirit, had been encouraged by his attendants to search for someone who could play the harp. (Harp music was said to have a soothing effect on a troubled spirit.) A servant knew of a son of Jesse who played the harp. And so Saul sent messengers to Jesse to summon my boy.

The soothing harp music worked, and Saul asked David to remain in his service. David continued to soothe Saul's spirit with his music, but he also went back and forth to tend his father's sheep in Bethlehem. I clung to the times he was with us and grieved at the times he was with Saul.

Time continued to pass and I saw less and less of David. His many feats were a great topic of conversation.

I heard of David's valor and courage in the slaying of the Philistine, Goliath. I was proud of him, but fear gripped my mother's heart when I imagined the dangers he would face as a warrior. I felt my son slipping away from me because I could no longer protect him.

And I wept for him.

I knew of David's close friendship with Jonathan, Saul's eldest son, and I was thankful for it, but I also worried. After all David had become Jonathan's rival for the crown and throne. I could no longer give him advice or help him with decisions. I was losing my son.

And I wept for him.

I heard also of David's failures and weaknesses and especially of his love for Bathsheba, who was another man's wife. I heard that he asked forgiveness from God, but I still worried. I felt so distant from him.

And I wept for him.

I saw how the Lord caused Israel to prosper under David's reign and that this was God's plan to create a dynasty that would last forever. So much responsibility for him! I ached for the man who had once been my baby boy.

And I wept for him and I wept for myself.

People talked of David's greatness and his heart for God, but I longed for my son and the closeness we had once shared. I grew older and my mind grew weak. As I closed my eyes in death, my last thoughts were of David, ruddy faced, freckles shining on his nose, hair windblown, running home from the fields with a lamb in his arms...

And now you.

Having someone you love leave your life can be heart wrenching. Sometimes the loss is gradual, as in the situation

David's mother faced, or sometimes the loss is abrupt. And it's something everyone will encounter to different degrees.

In our ever changing and fast moving world, it's very ordinary to become close friends with someone fate seems to have placed in your life. For a period of time your friendship and confidentiality grow until perhaps one day either you or your friend find that you must move to another area, sometimes far away. And as much as you try to remain close, it never seems the same. And you grieve for the friend.

Mothers who send their children off to school for the first time and mothers who sent their teens off to college often feel a keen sense of loss. As you bid your child farewell while trying to keep a stiff upper lip, inside your heart is breaking. And you grieve for your child.

Mothers and wives who say goodbye to a loved one who is entering the service of our country have a twofold dilemma. Not only are you faced with the loved one leaving you, but you are also faced with the fear that the loved one may be seriously injured or worse yet, may never return. And you grieve for your warrior.

And perhaps the most heart wrenching of all is losing your child, relative, or friend due to a circumstance out of your control or understanding. You try to make amends, you pray for God to intervene, but you continue to drift apart. When you reach the point where you have done all that you can possibly do, you just give the problem to God and keep the faith that someday, somehow, you'll be reconciled. In the meantime, you grieve for the one you love.

Whatever form your loss has taken, you can receive relief when you take your pain to God. He will listen and hold you in his arms and wipe away your tears. And he will answer your prayer although perhaps not in the way you would like. The answer may not come even in your lifetime, but be patient. God will provide.

> *God himself will be with them and be their God. He will wipe every tear from their eyes. There will be no more death or mourning or crying or pain* (Revelations 21:3-4).

So sometimes we just have to say goodbye, wipe away our tears, and wait for God to act. Be patient. God is a loving God and he knows how we feel. After all, he holds us in the palm of his hand, and he is and will always be there for us.

10

THE INNKEEPER'S WIFE

Accepting God's Gift to You
(Luke 2:1-20)

Hello. I come to you from long ago and far away. I would like to share with you an amazing event I experienced so many years ago. The event I experienced changed both the world and me.

I lived in Bethlehem of Judea, and it was census season in our country. Each male was required to return to the city of his birth and register as decreed by Caesar Augustus.

My husband and I owned an inn in Bethlehem, and census season was an extremely busy time for us. At the time I am sharing with you, our inn was overflowing with guests. It seemed as if every nook and cranny were filled. We housed old people, young people, children, babies, people from near and far. The noise was intense—babies crying, children yelling, arguments, disgruntled complaints—but, yes, there was laughter and merriment as well.

On the night of the amazing event I would like to share with you, most of the guests had settled down and all was mostly calm. I longed to go to my bedroom and crawl into my bed and rest my head on my pillow, but there was still so much for me to do. I had cooked so many meals, washed so many dishes, cleaned up so many messes, and I was feeling stressed and sorry for myself. As I finished scouring a pot in which the lamb stew had burned, I sat down to make a list of things I needed to remember for tomorrow and items I needed to purchase at the market. I was having trouble keeping my eyes open, but a knock at the door startled me. My instinct was to ignore the knock because I knew we had no room for any more guests.

But something tugged at my heart, and I opened the door to see two of the most pitiful looking people I had ever seen. He was young, dirty, and had a look of anguish and bewilderment on his face. She, appearing to be in her early teens, was seated on a donkey and seemed oh, so weary. She looked at me and smiled the most beautiful smile while I explained that we had absolutely no room at all, and they turned to leave. As they turned, I realized that she was with child, and most likely her time for delivery was very near.

Again something tugged at my heart, and I told the young man to go around back to our stable where my husband was taking care of the animals, and perhaps he might know of a vacancy.

I returned to my kitchen where I had at least two more hours of drudgery. I worked continually, still feeling sorry for myself, but I was almost finished when my husband came bursting through the door.

He had a big smile on his face, so I knew that nothing was wrong. He insisted that I come with him, right that minute, to the stable. I wanted to go to that smelly stable just about as much as I wanted to climb the fig tree in our yard and pick a basket of figs. I could almost hear my pillow calling me from my bedroom. However, he was so enthusiastic and happy that I grabbed my wrap and followed him.

The first thing I noticed when I stepped outside was how bright everything seemed. As I gazed up at the night sky, I was awed by a large, very bright star that seemed to be shining down directly on our stable!

Entering the stable, which was overcrowded by the animals of guests in addition to our animals, I stepped gingerly to avoid soiling my shoes. Even though the stable was smelly and nasty, calm seemed to prevail. All the animals, even the mice, were awake, but all were quiet.

It was then that I saw the couple I had sent to speak to my husband. They were in a corner on a bed of fresh straw that my husband must have provided. The man was still dirty, but his look of anguish and bewilderment had been replaced with a smile. She still looked weary, but her smile was even more beautiful than before. And then I saw the bundle in her arms. I was right! She had given birth to a child!

The baby was wrapped tightly and was sleeping peacefully. She motioned me to come nearer and asked if I would like to hold her son. As I took that child in my arms, I felt that tug at my heart again, and as I gazed at the face of the sleeping baby, I felt all sorts of emotions rush over me. I felt joy! I felt love! I felt peace! I felt hope! I felt calm! I felt happiness! I was no longer tired! I felt understanding, and then I realized that I was holding the Son of God in my arms, and my life would never be the same...

And now you.

You too will enter the season of Christmas. You may be expecting a house full of guests or you may be traveling far away. You have shopping, cleaning and decorating to do, cookies to make, menus to plan—the list seems endless, and each day more items and responsibilities seem to be added. The stress and anxiety may grow until all you want to do is to shut your bedroom door and rest your head on your pillow.

Before you become totally overwhelmed, you are encouraged to consider a few ideas. First of all, prioritize your list and don't try to do too much at one time. And most important of all, find some time *each day* for yourself. Stop, put aside all your planning, and focus on YOU. Have a cup of tea or coffee, thumb through a magazine, take a nap, read a chapter in that book you've been reading for two months, take a calming soak in the tub, listen to your favorite music, or perhaps just go sit in a comfy chair, wrap yourself in a warm afghan, and clear your mind of all the clutter. When you feel a wonderful sense of peace, close your eyes and imagine that young girl has just handed you her sleeping child to hold. Let emotions run over you. Feel love! Feel joy! Feel peace! Feel hope! Feel calm! Feel happiness! Then experience the understanding that because God gave you the gift you hold in your arms, your life will never be the same. Enjoy your season and have a merry Christmas!

> *For God so loved the world that he gave his one and only Son, that whoever believes in him shall not perish but have eternal life* (John 3:16).

Count your blessings! You never know who might knock at your door!

AND THE AFTER...

Writing these stories has been an amazing journey, and I have enjoyed each step of the way. I thank God for a good mind, for creative ideas, and for his book which he allowed me to use for inspiration.

The women of these stories, either unnamed or unmentioned, can hopefully speak to us today to offer encouragement and hope. Remembering that our loving God created us—man and woman—equally, let us take the experiences of these women (and the mistakes of Eve) to heal, to grow, and to move forward.

Thanks be to God.

About the Author

Although North Carolina is her birthplace, Ballwin, Missouri, where Marie Holt lives with her husband, Barry, is her home. Her profession as an educator has given her opportunities to work with students from kindergarten through the university level. St. Mark Presbyterian Church plays a major role in her life. There she is a deacon and an elder and has served as chair of several committees. Currently she is deeply involved with Stephen Ministry and other caregiving responsibilities.

CPSIA information can be obtained
at www.ICGtesting.com
Printed in the USA
FFOW05n1641120917

9 781581 696677